BEARPORT BIOGRAPHIES

JIMMY CARTER

PRESIDENT AND HUMANITARIAN

by Rachel Rose

Consultant: John Coleman, Professor of Political Science, University of Minnesota
Minneapolis, Minnesota

BEARPORT PUBLISHING

Minneapolis, Minnesota

Credits
Cover and title page, ©NurPhoto/Getty Images; 4, ©Everett Collection/Shutterstock; 5, ©Featureflash Photo Agency/Shutterstock; 7, ©Rabbani and Solimene Photography /Getty Images; 8, ©Kit Leong/Shutterstock; 9, ©Matthew Simmons /Getty Images; 10, ©Kevin Stuart /Getty Images; 12, ©Richard Cartwright /Getty Images; 14, ©Joe Seer/Shutterstock; 15, ©DFree/Shutterstock; 16, ©Save the Children/Flickr; 17, ©Mike Coppola /Getty Images; 18, ©Noam Galai/Getty Images; 19, ©GASTON DE CARDENAS/Getty Images; 20, © Allstar Picture Library Ltd. /Alamy; 21, ©Leon Bennett/Getty Images

President: Jen Jenson
Director of Product Development: Spencer Brinker
Editor: Allison Juda

Library of Congress Cataloging-in-Publication Data

Names: Rose, Rachel, 1968- author.
Title: Jimmy Carter : president and humanitarian / by Rachel Rose.
Other titles: President and humanitarian
Description: Minneapolis, Minnesota : Bearport Publishing Company, [2021] | Series: Bearport biographies | Includes bibliographical references and index.
Identifiers: LCCN 2020039233 (print) | LCCN 2020039234 (ebook) | ISBN 9781647477172 (library binding) | ISBN 9781647477257 (paperback) | ISBN 9781647477332 (ebook)
Subjects: LCSH: Carter, Jimmy, 1924---Juvenile literature. | Presidents--United States--Biography--Juvenile literature. | Human rights workers--United States--Biography--Juvenile literature.
Classification: LCC E873 .R67 2021 (print) | LCC E873 (ebook) | DDC 973.926092 [B]--dc23
LC record available at https://lccn.loc.gov/2020039233
LC ebook record available at https://lccn.loc.gov/2020039234

For more information, write to Bearport Publishing, 5357 Penn Avenue South, Minneapolis, MN 55419.
Printed in the United States of America

Contents

The Nobel Peace Prize

Every seat of the beautiful city hall in Oslo, Norway, was filled, and the crowd was excited. They were all there to see former U.S. President Jimmy Carter receive a great honor. Jimmy had won the Nobel Peace Prize for his many years of work bringing peace and human rights to people around the world.

Jimmy's Nobel Prize

Jimmy accepted his Nobel Peace Prize on December 10, 2002.

Jimmy Carter was the third U.S. president to receive the Nobel Peace Prize.

From Peanuts to Politics

James Earl Carter Jr. was born on October 1, 1924. Jimmy, as he was known, grew up on his family's peanut farm in Plains, Georgia. When Jimmy was young, his uncle Tom was in the U.S. Navy. Tom sent his family postcards from around the world. Young Jimmy got a **glimpse** of life outside the farm, and he knew he wanted to join the navy, too.

Jimmy graduated from the U.S. Naval Academy in 1946. He served in the navy for the next seven years.

Jimmy on the family peanut farm

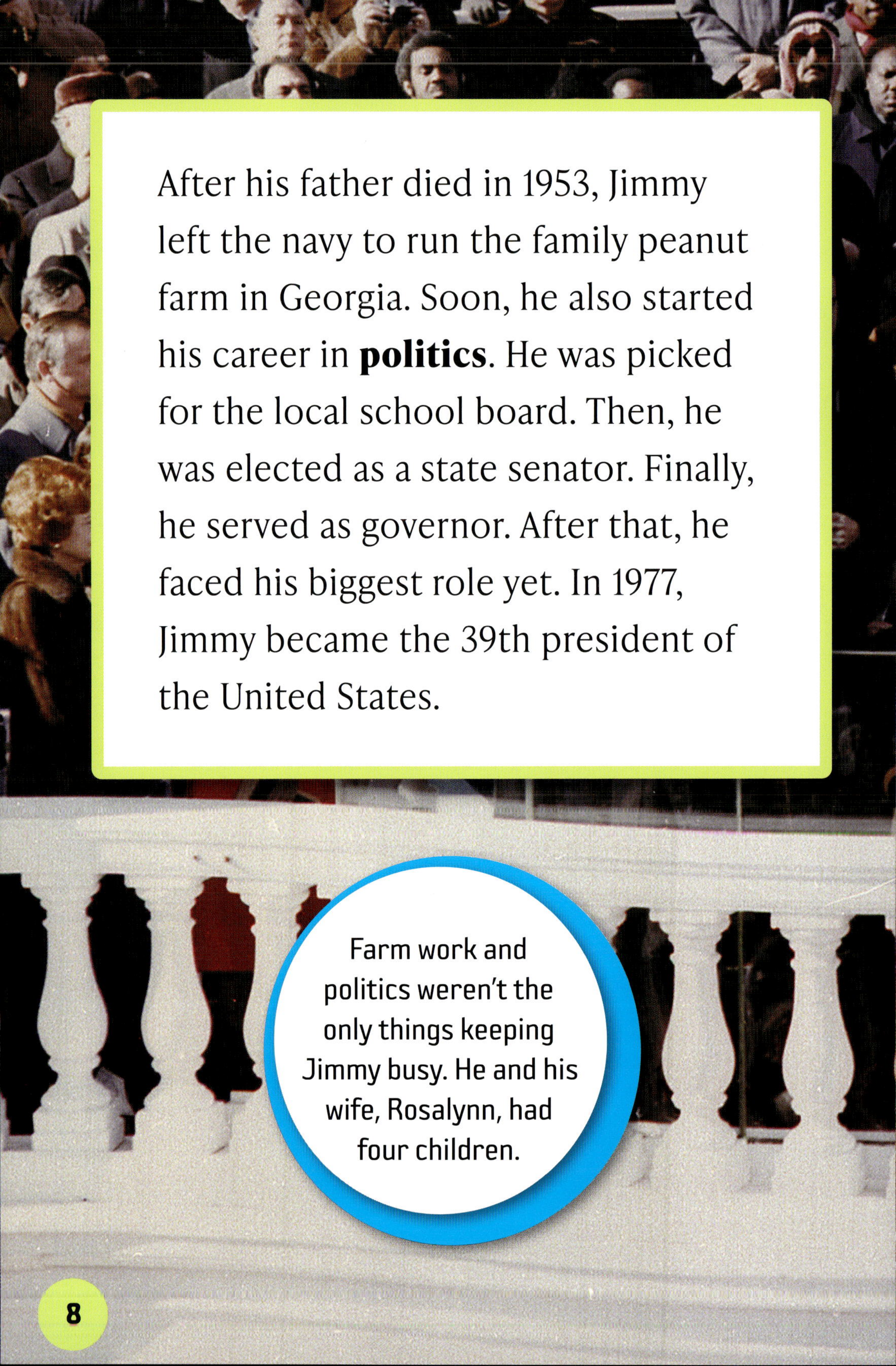

After his father died in 1953, Jimmy left the navy to run the family peanut farm in Georgia. Soon, he also started his career in **politics**. He was picked for the local school board. Then, he was elected as a state senator. Finally, he served as governor. After that, he faced his biggest role yet. In 1977, Jimmy became the 39th president of the United States.

Farm work and politics weren't the only things keeping Jimmy busy. He and his wife, Rosalynn, had four children.

Jimmy *(middle right)* as he became president

Presidential Ups and Downs

One of Jimmy's shining moments as president was when he helped bring peace between Israel and Egypt. The countries had been at war for many years. In 1978, the heads of these countries met with each other and Jimmy at Camp David. He helped them **negotiate** a peace agreement.

Camp David

Camp David is the presidential country **residence** in Maryland.

Egyptian President Anwar Sadat *(left)* and Jimmy at Camp David.

Students in Iran climbed the walls of the U.S. embassy to break in.

Two U.S. military helicopters crashed on their way to save the embassy hostages. This ended the rescue early.

Jimmy also faced many challenges as president. In 1979, a group of students took over the U.S. **embassy** in Iran and held 66 Americans **hostage**. Jimmy tried hard to free the hostages. Eventually, he even called for the U.S. military to rescue the hostages, but the mission failed. Soon, Jimmy's first presidential **term** was up. He faced off against Ronald Reagan for president and lost. Jimmy left the White House in 1981.

Peace, Rights, Health, and Homes

During his presidency, Jimmy wanted to bring peace to the world. He continued this **humanitarian** work after he left the White House. In 1982, Jimmy and Rosalynn opened the Carter Center in Atlanta, Georgia. The center has **programs** that help peace efforts in over 80 countries. It also helps countries make their voting systems fair.

The Carter Center

When he was the president, Jimmy made August 26 "Women's Equality Day."

The Carter Center has many projects aimed to help improve women's lives.

The Carter Center runs many health programs, too. One of them works to stop the spread of Guinea worm **disease**, which is spread through dirty drinking water. In 1986, there were over 3.5 million cases of the disease. Jimmy knew that he needed to do something. The Carter Center worked with local communities to help fix the problem. In 2019, there were only 54 cases worldwide!

Jimmy speaks to children in Sudan about Guinea worm disease.

Guinea worm disease is a very painful disease that causes **blisters** on the body.

Jimmy counted down the years until Guinea worm disease was gone.

Since it first began in 1976, Habitat for Humanity has helped over 29 million people build or improve their homes.

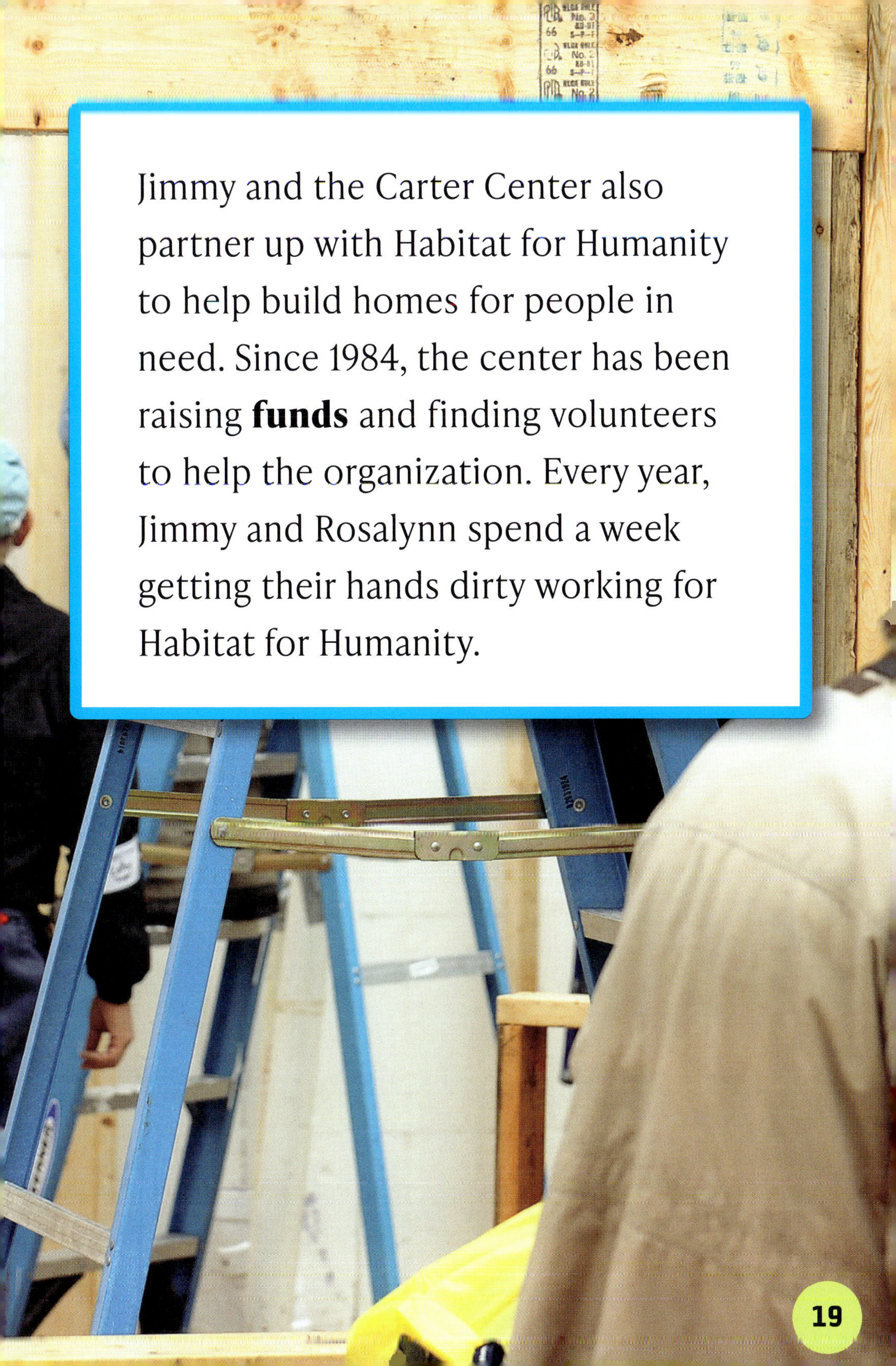

Jimmy and the Carter Center also partner up with Habitat for Humanity to help build homes for people in need. Since 1984, the center has been raising **funds** and finding volunteers to help the organization. Every year, Jimmy and Rosalynn spend a week getting their hands dirty working for Habitat for Humanity.

Living with Purpose

Whether running a country or running an organization, Jimmy Carter's purpose has always been to build peace throughout the world. He cares deeply about people. Jimmy wants to be remembered as a president who did his best for his country and who was a champion for peace and human rights.

Jimmy Carter is America's longest-living president.

Timeline

Here are some key dates in Jimmy Carter's life.

1924
Born on October 1

1953
Leaves the navy

1977
Becomes president

1982
Opens the Carter Center

2002
Wins the Nobel Peace Prize

2012
Travels to Haiti with Habitat for Humanity

2020
Helps erase Guinea worm disease

Glossary

blisters raised spots on the skin that are caused by an injury or illness

disease an illness or sickness

embassy a place where people who are from one country live or work in another country

funds money raised for a special purpose

glimpse a brief look at something

hostage a person held prisoner by someone who demands that something be done before the person is set free

humanitarian a person who works to improve the lives and living conditions of other people

negotiate to talk about something in order to come to an agreement

politics the activities, actions, and plans that are used to gain and hold power in a government

programs plans to get things done

residence a house or place where someone lives

term the amount of time an official has to serve in office

Index

Read More

Elston, Heidi M. D. *Jimmy Carter (The United States Presidents)*. Minneapolis: Abdo Publishing, 2020.

Hobkirk, Lori. *James Earl Carter (The United States Presidents)*. Mankato, MN: The Child's World, 2020

Learn More Online

1. Go to **www.factsurfer.com**
2. Enter "**Jimmy Carter**" into the search box.
3. Click on the cover of this book to see a list of websites.

About the Author

Rachel Rose is a writer who lives in San Francisco. Her favorite books to write are about people who lead inspiring lives.